INDEX

(Song titles differing from first lines are in ita

1. Are You Ready For the Action

(Shaping Up)

DAVE COOKE

G F C F G F
keep our -selves to - geth - er no mat - ter what the weath
C F G F C F
- her You may be light as a feath - er or
C D C D G F
hea - vy as lead with a great big head but it rea - lly does - n't mat
C F G D Em C G D
- ter when it comes to shap - ing up when it comes to shap - ing up

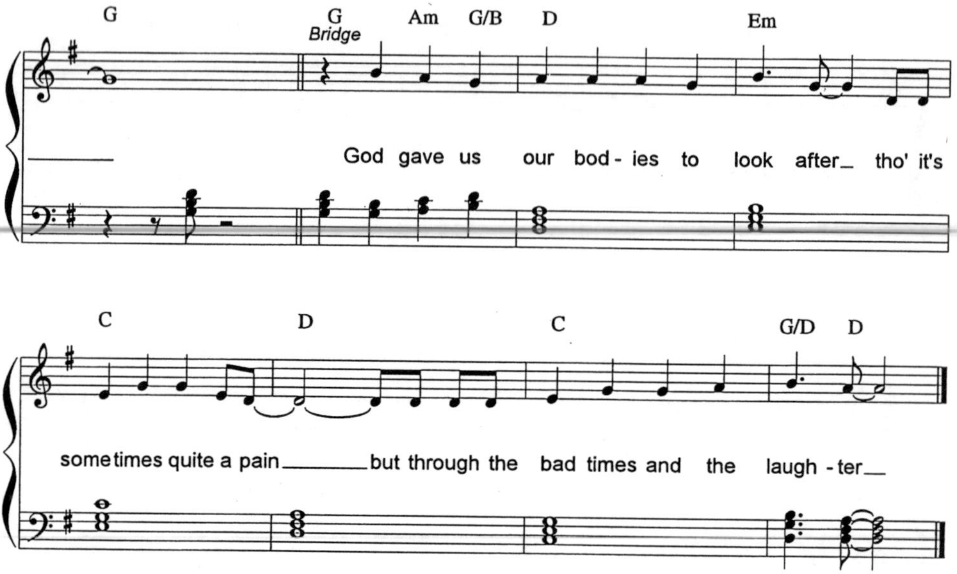

Actions verse 1

It's good to run and cycle and swim
And walk and step and visit the gym
And do those weights, play tennis and squash
Play football, rugby, eat healthy nosh
Throw that javelin, hit that ball
Do those press-ups, fifty in all
Row that boat, swing that bat,
Learn to become an acrobat
There's never never never enough
When it comes to shaping up
When it comes to shaping up

Actions verse 2

Do a star jump then clap your hands
Run on the spot then jump
Shake a friend's hand to the left then the right
And hands above the head and clap three times
Take a deep breath and hold it in
Then let it out with a noise
Hands on your head and down to your toes
Then stretch to the sky and jump

NOTES:
Another song that is hard to interpret completely in score model!! As you will see, I have tried to include all the main sung parts of the song in notation, chords etc., though it's pointless bar counting the rap action sections. You can work that out from the track, or make up you own!! Easy vamping on the chord of G, or use the progression G F C F as a means of linking the sections will be effective. A useful tip is to get someone on the stage to dance through the actions and lead with all the ups and downs. If done correctly, it's a great sweaty one!!

ROCKY KIDS
RK

2. Here's The Bible

(Bible In One Song)

DAVE COOKE

♩=93

G D A D G D G D
two books of Kings and two books of Chron-i-cles Ez-ra Ne-he-mi-ah Es-ther Jo - b and
G A D G A D
a hun-dred and fifty Psalms A hun - dred_ and fifty Psalms so
(How many?)
G F#7 Bm7 Gm6
learn as you go that's all you go - tta do_ Just
D C/E G/D A D
close your eyes start to re - vise the books in the old and the books in the new

Here's the Bible in one song
There's nothing left out so sing along
It starts with the Old and ends with the New
So learn as you go that's all you gotta do.

In the beginning was Genesis and Exodus
Followed by Leviticus, and Numbers
1 2 3 4 5 Deuteronomy
Joshua, Judges, Ruth.

Up comes Samuel One and Two
Then Two books of Kings and Two books of Chronicles
Ezra, Nehemiah, Esther, Job
And 150 psalms - how many?150 Psalms!!

So learn as you go, that's all you gotta do
Close your eyes, start to revise
The books in the Old and the books in the New

Several hundred Proverbs, if you please
And tales of woe from Ecclesiastes
Solomon's spicy Song of Songs
Isaiah, Jeremiah, then Lamentations.

Ezekiel and Daniel
Hosea, Joel and Amos
Obadiah, Jonah, and his whale
Not forgetting all the lions in the Daniel tale.

Micah (whose car?) Micah!! Nahum
Habakkuk, Zephaniah
Haggai (what a guy) Zechariah
And right at the end there's Malachi

How many books can you count in the Old
And how many in the New?
Add them together it's 66
Count as you go that's all you gotta do

So learn as you go, that's all you gotta do
Close your eyes, start to revise
The books in the Old and the books in the New

Matthew, Mark, Luke and John,
Acts and Romans follow on
Letters to Corinthians 1 and 2
That talk about the things we ought to do.

There's a letter to Galatians, and a letter to Ephesians
If there's not enough work for the postman to do
There's one to Phillipians and one to Colossians
And Two to the chaps called Thessalonians.

So learn as you go, that's all you gotta do
Close your eyes, start to revise
The books in the Old and the books in the New

Two letters to Timothy arrive on time
Then Titus and Philemon
A letter to the Hebrews and another from James
All delivered by a very tired postman.

Peter writes a couple and sticks them in the box
Then up pops John with a 1,2,3
Then a little bit of wisdom from a guy called Jude
And it's all a Revelation.

That's the Bible in one song
With nothing left out it's a little bit long
39 in the Old, 27 in the New
Learn by heart, that's all you got to do

So learn as you go, that's all you gotta do
Close your eyes, start to revise
The books in the Old and the books in the New

NOTES:

The most impossible song to write out!! I think that had I scored the entire song, It would have taken up an additional volume and caused the publishers total grief. So I have scored the first part, up to the bridge. The music scored generally represents all the music in the song and it's a simple case of fitting in the lyrics using the basic chords of D C G and A. As this is meant to be a learning song to remember all the books in the Bible, then my defence is that you must also learn it!! A couple of times from the CD should do the trick!!

ROCKY KIDS
RK

3. Hey Hey We're The Rocky Kids

(Rocky Kids)

DAVID COOKE

NOTES

Although this is the key on the album track, you can Capo the first fret for guitar and play it in A, or Capo 3rd fret and play it in G, which is much easier.
I haven't written the entire song here including all the instrumental bits so simply play along with your air guitar until you recognise where you are!! You must play this with loads of energy.

4. I'm Feeling Moody

(Joy Joy Joy)

♩=135

TRAD
ARR. DAVE COOKE

2. I'm feeling angry, and I've had a row,
One with my Mum,
One with my Dad, and one with the dog
I'm feeling angry, and I've had a row with everyone else
Life is a total pain.

3. I just don't feel like being nice right now
So please go away,
Please go away, please go away
I just don't feel like being nice right now, so please go away
Go away right now.

4. I've got no friends and no one likes me
OOO what a shame
O what a shame, O what a shame
I've got no friends and no one likes me,
OOO what a shame
It's such a terrible shame.

5. We've got to ask God to forgive us, when?
Starting right now,
Starting right now, starting right now
We've got to ask God to forgive us, when?
starting right now
Starting right away.

6. I've got to start forgiving other people, starting today
Starting today, starting today
I've got to start forgiving other people, starting today
Starting right away.

7. I'm feeling better now I've said I'm sorry,
O what a change
O what.a change, O what a change
I'm feeling better now I've said I'm sorry, O what a change
O what a change in me.

8. I'll be a friend to you and you and you
I hope that's alright, I hope that's alright
I'll be a friend to you and you and you, I hope that's alright
I hope that's alright with you.

9. I've got the love of God deep down in my heart, where?
Down in my heart, where? Down in my heart
I've got the love of God deep down in my heart.
Glory to His name

10. I've got that peace that passes understanding,
Down in my heart, where?
Down in my heart, where? Down in my heart
I've got that peace that passes understanding down in my heart
Glory to His name

11. I've got that Joy Joy Joy, Joy down in my heart, where?
Down in my heart, where? Down in my heart
I've got that Joy Joy Joy Joy down in my heart
Glory to His name (repeat)

NOTES:
A great stomp this one. If you can't find a good drum loop to play this one to, then get everyone to stamp, clap, and bang something in time.This also works really well with a few dancers at the front leading some serious leaping about! Chose the best key for you to start in and allow for the key changes.

5. I've Got A Reason To Celebrate

DAVE COOKE &
PAUL FIELD

2. Sometimes you feel like you don't fit in
You're afraid of getting left behind
But just remember where love begins
To God you are a winner every time.

6. I Will Walk

(Captain Of My Soul)

DAVE COOKE &
JUDY MACKENZIE DUNN

A E B
tell me to come I will rest when You tell me to rest_ 'cos it's
C♯m A F♯m B
You who loves me best.
Chorus
A² E
'cos You're the cap - tain of my soul
B A²
You are the one who's

E
B
in con - trol____ I've put my
F♯m
A
B
F♯m
A
life in to Your hands____ and I will foll - ow Your com - mands
B
A²
B
____ 'cos You're the cap - tain__ of my__
E
soul.____

ROCKY KIDS
RK

7. Is Your Inside Like Your Outside

(Inside Outside)

DAVE COOKE &
JUDY MACKENZIE DUNN

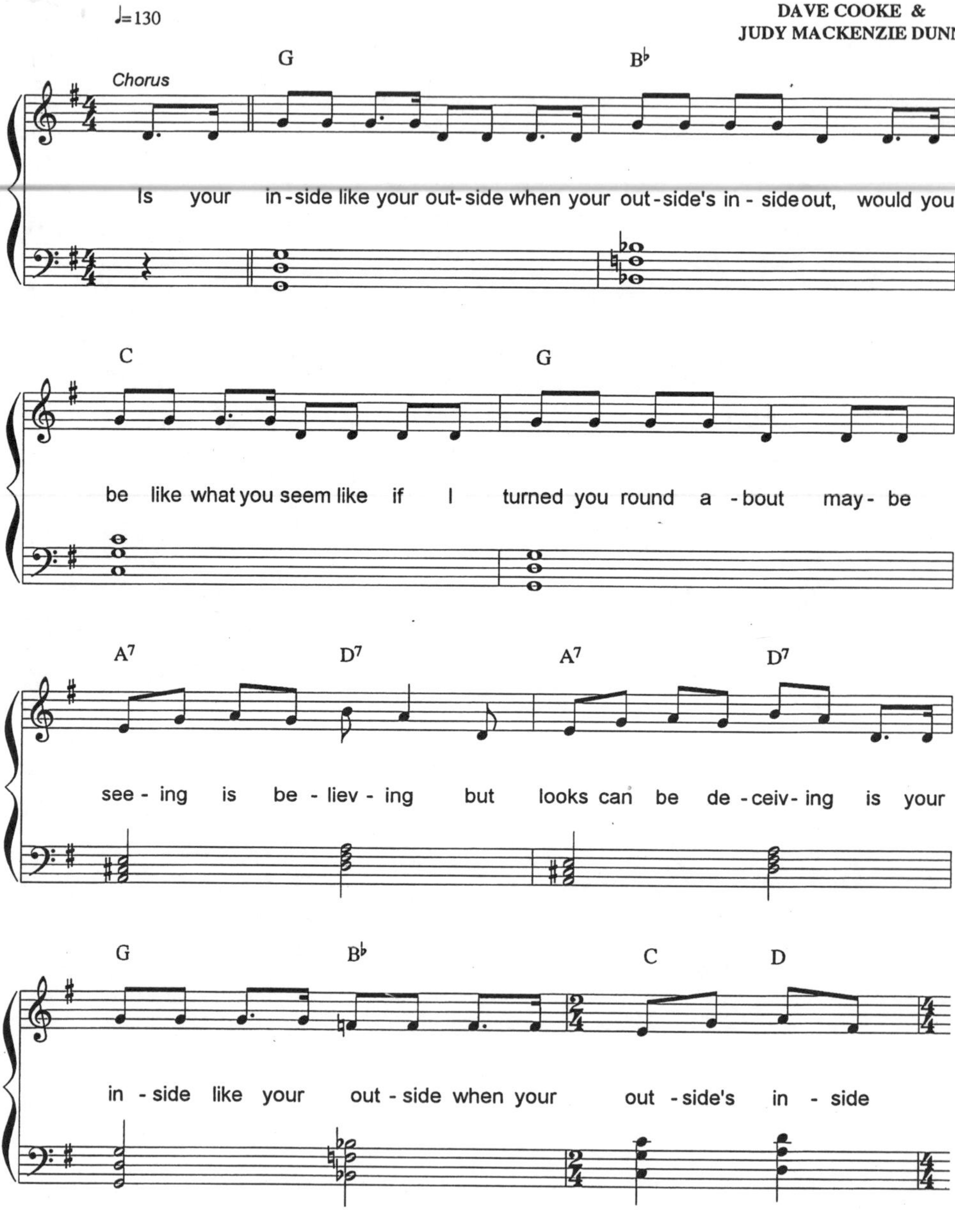

G
Verse 1
out.
And it
D7
G
D7
re-ally does-n't mat-ter how you look to me there's more to you than
G
C
A/C#
I can see I know as far as I'm con-cer-ned
G/D
B/D#
Em
A7
D7
some - times we are not what we ap-pear to be

2. And I wonder what we're thinking
   When we all shake hands
   Does it really mean that we're
   The best of friends
   Even though I smile politely
   Sometimes I've got
   Something else on my mind

3. Long and lumpy short and stumpy
   Fat or thin
   It's hard to tell the kind of
   State you're in
   Who is this person hiding
   Underneath your skin
   That's what I want to know.

4. Would you recognise me when I'm
   In disguise
   Tell me how I'm feeling by the
   Look in your eyes
   If you could read my mind then you'd
   Get a surprise
   I hope you'd understand it.

ROCKY KIDS
RK

8. Jesus And His Friends

♩=160

DAVE COOKE

Final verse
E D A E
And the rain stopped fal - ling and the sea be-came still, And the
E F♯m B
thun - der and the light - ning blew a - way And
E D A E
Je - sus kept tal - king to the storm un - til He
F♯m B E
♩=160
turned it to the brigh - test day In the

2. Now the sky grew dark and the wind began to blow
And the water all around was doing quick quick slow
and the men in the boat were getting quite scared
But Jesus stayed asleep and seemed unaware
Of the storm on the water
In the boat on the water

3. Now the sky was black and the thunder roared
And the men were throwing everything overboard
And the noise grew louder and louder and louder
And the boat began to sink and take on water
And His friends began to scream and cry for help
When Jesus woke up and shouted STOP!!!

NOTES:
It is obvious when listening to this song on the album that verse three is longer than the other verses. The lines simply turn round on the sequence E D A E and finishing on a loud E on the words 'STOP!'. The sound effects for verse 3 can be anything that suggests thunder, water and sounds that get louder and louder. It's a great thing to rehearse the final 'Stop' so all the sounds finishes together. Then play the final verse very quietly, reprising the 'In the boat' lines back to the original tempo.

Again I haven't included all the links for the verses. This is a simple turn round on the four chords E D A E.

ROCKY KIDS
RK

9. Jesus Loves Me

TRAD
ARR. DAVE COOKE

♩=165

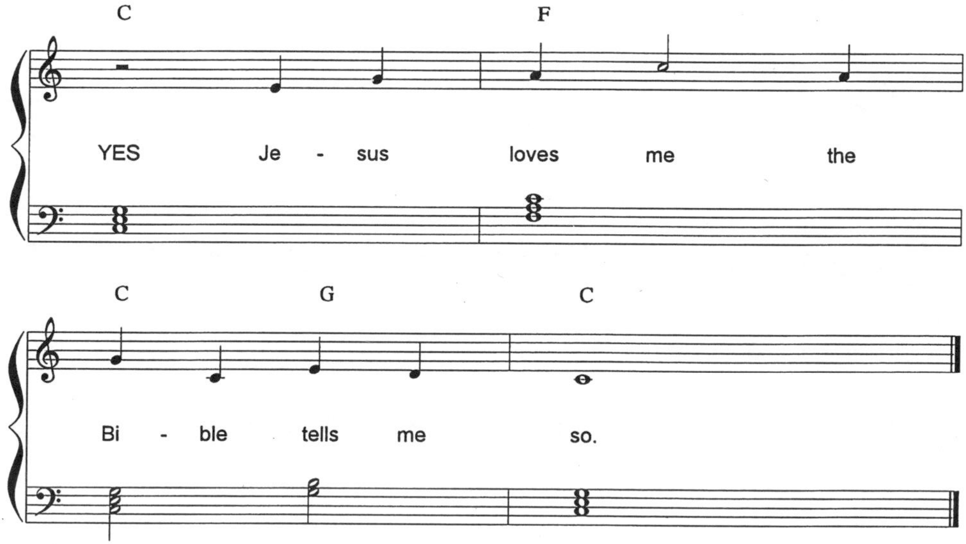

2. Jesus is a friend of mine,
He is with me all the time,
Even when I'm feeling down,
He is there I'm not alone.

No!! He'll not leave me
No!! He'll not leave me
No!! He'll not leave me
The Bible tells me so.

3. God the Father He's OK
Jesus came to show the way
The Holy Spirit guides us through
Picks us up when we're feeling blue

YES YES YES He loves me
YES YES YES He loves me
YES YES YES He loves me
The Bible tells me so

NOTES:
This song can go in many ways. On the album I have done it quite gently, with a sort of African rhythm but it's just as good in a Rocky style. Make sure that the 'Shouts' in all the choruses are very LOUD!! You can even get a very good Mexican wave going if when they shout they stand up as well!!

10. One Two Three Four

DAVE COOKE

F♯
E
four five six sev - en
one day we're gon - na be in heav - en
A
five six sev - en eight
B
it's great no need to hes - i - tate no need to
con - cen - trate no need to make a date time to ap -

pre - ci - ate, just take Him at His word ac - cept that
B A C#m B E
Je - sus is Lord six seven eight nine
we'll have lots of time
F#
sev - en eight nine ten

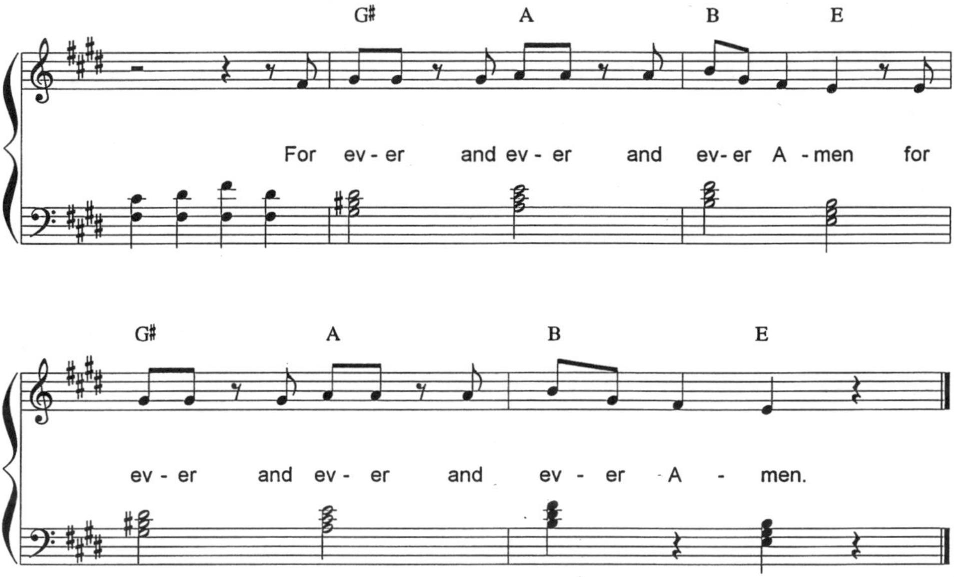

NOTES:

All attempts to write down a simple rock and roll piano were virtually impossible. Apolgies for the rather stilted flavour of this but it gives you an idea. Just let it all go. Forget the music and play the blues. I know that had I tried to transcribe the piano on the track it would have appeared as though several large flies and their friends had been terribly ill after a rather dubious curry the night before!!! I think you get the picture??!

11. The Bird Needs The Worm

(All Works Together)

PAUL FIELD &
DAVE COOKE

D6 C#7 F#m G#m A A/B
praise to God_ the King_ For He made ev-ery liv-ing thing_ to work to-geth
E C D
Bridge
-er_________ (The) Ev - ery liv - ing thing_ has a
E C D
spe - cial part to play_ it all goes wrong if you
E A E/G#
take a piece a-way_ so learn to see_ the won-der in cre -

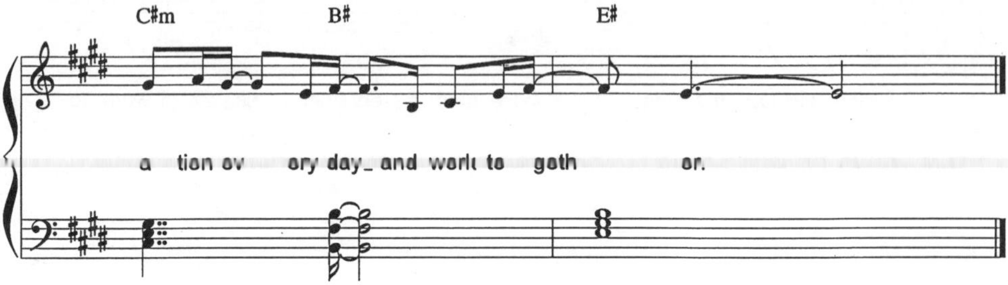

3. It's all up to you and it's all up to me
There's no one else to blame so try to see that
Caring for the world it's gotta be
So it all works together

NOTES :

On all of these songs I have not scored all the instrumental intros, outros, solos, and bridges. It is very possible that you will want to make up your own introductions to these when you play them on either solo piano or guitar. This one works simply playing E to Esus4 in the correct tempo as an intro and link to each section.

ROCKY KIDS
RK

12. The Tongue Is A Funny Old Thing

(Tongue Song)

DAVE COOKE

G D Bm7 E9 A
tongue is a fun - ny old thing, The tongue is a fun-ny old
D D Bm
Verse
thing. With our tongue we shout bad words
G A
with our tongue we praise the Lord, We
G D Bm
curse and we swear and we don't seem to care that our

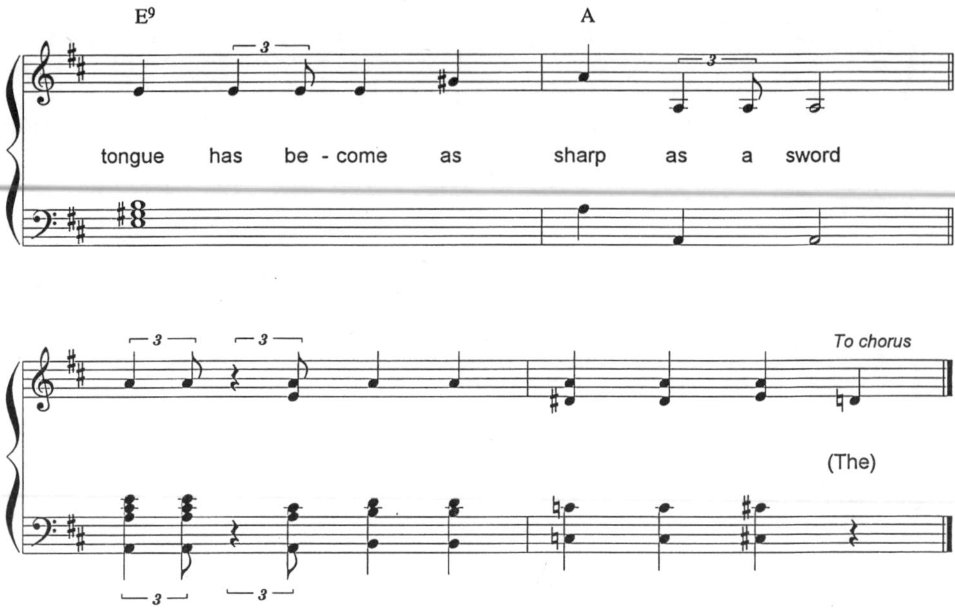

2. It's a spark that sets the forest ablaze
The tongue is poison in loads of ways
We shout and we Huzzle....
And we moan and we Gruzzle....
Then from the same place come shouts of praise
Hallelujah!!

Bridge

```
          G          A      D
Can an apple tree grow bananas? No!!
          G          A      D
Does an egg plant grow tomates No!!
          G                D
We must learn to tame out tongues right now
     A              D
And ask for God to show us how
          G                D
We must learn to tame our tongues right now
     A              D    G  D
And ask for God to show us how
```

Tongue twister RAP

Try a tongue twister mister
Get your tongue at the ready steady
Say the things that are good to say and fade away
The bad words, naughty words
Fill your head with God's word
That's what we've gotta do Yes!! That's right!!

ROCKY KIDS
RK

13. We Don't Want No Pumpkin's Head

(We've Got Jesus)

DAVE COOKE

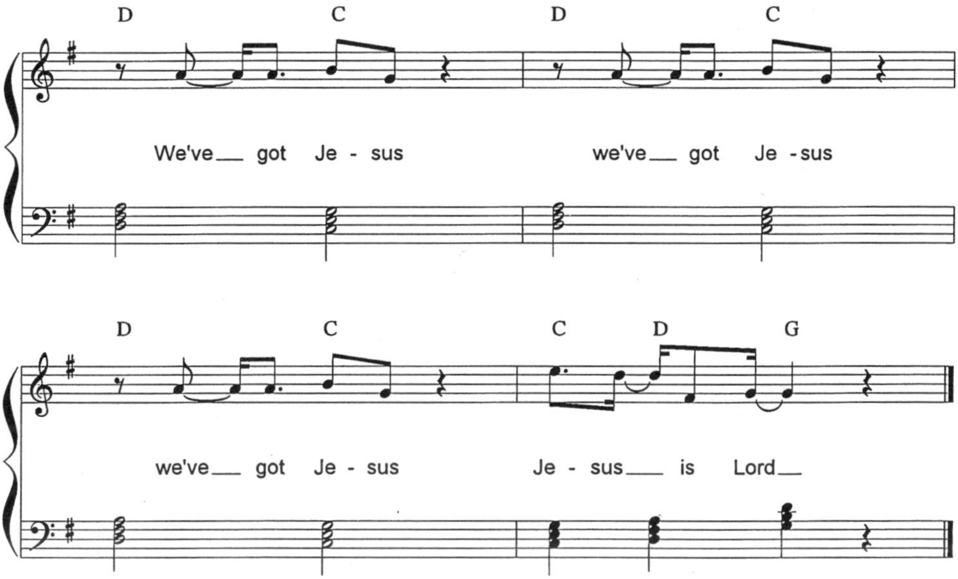

2. We've no time for casting spells
Trick and treat is a no no
Wizards and ghouls and giants that smell
And Halloween stories on the video 'cos

3. We don't want no pointed hats
Or hitching a ride on a broomstick
We've no time for vampire bats
Even when you've eaten loads of garlic

4. We don't need a trick or treat
Howling wolves are an earful
Frankenstein look alikes with great big feet
None of this is gonna make us fearful 'cos

Bridge
Some people want to do it
Some people want to be scared
But we've gotta better thing going on
You want to know why?

NOTES:
A very useful little song for Halloween night. Specially good for getting rid of unwanted spooks. Fling open those doors of hte church and shout 'Jesus is Lord'... then listen to the stampede!!! A good idea for this song is to establish the rhythm using the on beat with the feet, and the off beat with claps, so beats 1 & 3 will be feet stomps, and 2 & 4 claps. It's very powerful, and great to play to, sepecially if you have a whole stack of people doing it!! To be used throughout the year, not just the 31st October!

CHORD HINT: G/5 is the chord of G without the 3rd note (B). This means you can play it with a 'bluesy' feel as well.

14. Well I Never Could Fly

(Fly Like An Eagle)

DAVE COOKE &
JUDY MACKENZIE-DUNN

2. Well I never could run like a racehorse
'Cos I don't have four legs
And I never could cluck like a chicken
And I'll never lay an egg
And I never could eat like a pelican can
With one enormous beak (Throw me a sardine!!)
But I can walk with Jesus.....

3. Well I never could drink like an elephant
'Cos I don't have a trunk
And I never could look like an aardvark
Or smell just like a skunk
And I never could snap like a crocodile
'Cos I don't have sharp teeth (Gimme the mouthwash)
But I can walk with Jesus....

NOTES:

Nice and easy feel this one: Play it Capo 4 in C if that's a bit easier. The 'Have a Banana' lines are meant to be a very loud Shout, and so build up the verses so when you get to that point you are ready to YELL!!